Small Graces

Small Graces

A collection of family devotions, lest we lose sight
Of the joy of simple expressions
Of love, thankfulness, and a sense of
God's presence in our daily lives.

Written and Compiled
by Anne Sandall

Linocut Illustrations
by Diane Sandall

SOLSIDAN HOUSE
BOOKS & FINE ART

Published by Solsidan House

SOLSIDAN HOUSE
BOOKS & FINE ART

475 SUNNYSIDE DRIVE EUGENE, OREGON 97404

Printed in the U.S.A.
First Edition

Library of Congress Control Number: 2004095176

ISBN 0-9741620-1-9

Printed by: Pease Bindery, Lincoln, NE

Our Personal Acknowledgments

Thanks are due to the following for their unfailing support, their belief in the importance of this project, their help, friendship and prayers, and for the joy they have taken as we have walked down this new path

Bob Sandall, patient husband and father, proof reader and cheerleader

Iris and Alden, beloved children and grandchildren who were the gentlest of art critics and patient beyond their years when art duties called

The Reverend Aaron Manderbach, DD, for reading our manuscript in its early stages and providing comments and a Foreword

The Reverend Donald Armstrong for his encouragement to go forward

Sharon Green, editor, friend and source of information about things we didn't even know we needed to know

Barbara Ann Swanson, book design, computer assistance, and typesetter

Erin Seligman for her help with the hymn

Bishop Alpha Mohamed, Rift Valley Diocese, Tanzania for whom we created a Swahili version after he and his family translated the manuscript; and without whom I might have lost faith and courage to finish the book. The joy and friendship I have known in working with him is beyond telling; he is truly God's servant.

Friends and family everywhere who have added prayers to use, lent us encouragement, and cheered for a successful outcome for our endeavor

Dedication

This work is dedicated to
My daughters
And Grandchildren
Who have taught me more about
Thankfulness and Joy
Than all the words in all the books
I have ever read.
Thank you all.
A.S.

To my beloved,
To my muse, and
To my favorite companions:
Blessings and Peace.
D.S.

Author's Statement

Let these small Thanksgivings inform the hearts
Of all who
Read, Hear, and Pray them.

Anne Sandall

O Lord, in your Holy Spirit,
Give us each an inquiring and discerning heart,
The courage to will and to persevere,
A spirit to know and to love you,
And the gift of joy and wonder
In all your works.

Book of Common Prayer 1979

Oh Lord, that lends me life,
Lend me a heart repleat with thankfulness.

William Shakespeare
England 1564–1616

Foreword

Anne Sandall and her daughter, Diane, have compiled a grand and useful collection of prayers that are meaningfully illustrated. This book can help parents, teachers, and even older sisters and brothers to introduce small, young people to the life of the Spirit. Several years ago, when searching for a book of prayers to put in the hands of parents who were seeking help for their pre-school son, I would have welcomed this slim volume. Its rhythms and rhymes make these prayers accessible and memorable, a foundation on which to build and to grow.

I would like to make a small addition to the content of the book. This little Creed was among "Household Prayers—A Child's Faith" in the Forward Movement's "Prayers—New and Old."

> I believe in God above,
> I believe in Jesus' love,
> I believe His Spirit too,
> Comes to teach me what to do.
> I believe that I can be
> True and loving, Lord, like Thee.

It is a privilege to commend "Small Graces," compiled by a mother and daughter team who were members, some years ago, of Saint Stephen's Church, Ridgefield, Connecticut. May it be an instrument to enable more and more of God's children to draw closer to Him and one another.

The Rev. Aaron Manderbach, DD
Meadow Ridge, Redding, Connecticut

Contents

Lord of all hopefulness, Lord of all joy,
Whose trust, ever childlike, no cares could destroy,
Be there at our waking, and give us, we pray,
Your bliss in our hearts, Lord, at the break of the day.

Jan Struther
1933

Good Morning God
The Break of the Day

With humble heart and tongue,
Our God, to Thee we pray,
Oh, make us learn while we are young,
How we may cleanse our way.

Make us, unguarded youth,
The objects of Thy care,
Help us to choose the way of truth
And fly from every snare.

Our hearts, to folly prone,
Renew by power divine;
Unite them to Thyself alone,
And make us wholly Thine.

Oh, let Thy word of grace
Our warmest thoughts employ;
Be thus through all our following days
Our treasure and our joy.

To what Thy laws impart,
Be our whole soul inclined;
Oh, let them dwell within our heart,
And sanctify our mind.

This morning, God, this is your day.
I am your child;
Show me your way.

Iona Community
Scotland

Dear Father, hear and bless
Thy beasts and singing birds;
And guard with tenderness,
Small things that have no words.

Traditional

O God, make us children of quietness
And heirs of peace.
Amen

St. Clement

Jesus, hold my hand today,
Guide my footsteps while I play.
From morning till its time to sleep,
Make me gentle, kind, and sweet.
Amen

Anne Sandall

God made the world so broad and grand,
Filled with blessings from
His hand.
He made the sky so high and blue,
And all the little children too.

Traditional

My God was with me all the night
And gave me sweet repose;
His angels watched me while I slept
Or I had never rose.
Now for the mercies of the night
My humble thanks I'll pay,
And unto God I'll dedicate
The first fruits of the day.

O God, Creator of light: at the rising
Of your sun this morning, let the greatest
Of all light, your love,
Rise like the sun within our hearts.

Armenian Apostolic Church Lebanon

Parable of the Sower

Many people had come together out of every city, hoping to hear Jesus teach. He told them a story—also known as a parable. Jesus frequently told stories to help people understand just what he was trying to teach them.

> A farmer went out to sow his seed and as he was spreading it, some fell by the wayside where it was stepped on and eaten by the birds. Other fell on the rocks where, as soon as it sprouted, it withered for lack of water. Some fell in the thorns and weeds and when it sprouted, it was overrun by the weeds and was choked. But some of the seed fell on good ground and sprouted and grew strong and bore fruit by the hundreds. His disciples didn't quite understand the point of the story so Jesus explained it.

> The seed is the word of God; the seeds along the wayside are people who hear but the word of God is taken out of their hearts and no good comes. The seeds that fall on the rocks are the people who hear and receive the word of God, but it does not take root and in time of temptation, they fall away from believing. Those which fell among weeds and thorns are like people who hear God's word, and go out and are choked with cares and riches of this world and bring no good fruit. The seeds that fall on good ground are people who are honest, have good hearts, hear the word, and keep it, and patiently bring forth good fruit.

I think we are meant to hear God's word, keep it, share it, and patiently bring good to the world.

He prayeth best, who loveth best
All things both great and small;
For the dear God who loveth us,
He made and loveth all.

Samuel Taylor Coleridge
England 1772–1834
The Rime of the Ancient Mariner

Dear God in Paradise
Look upon our sowing;
Bless the little gardens
And the green things growing.

Unknown

Oh Lord, I love all those who love you;
With their hands they have served you;
With their thoughts they have designed good things;
They have made this earth
To be a good place to live.
Thank you Lord.
Amen

Bishop Alpha Mohamed

God, who has made this land so beautiful,
Fill me with a love of her mountains and rivers,
Plains and deserts, fertile lands and meadows,
Woodland paths and streams
That I may care for them according to your will
And cherish and preserve them
For our time and for all who will
Follow on this loving path.
Amen

Anne Sandall

Our Father, who art in heaven,
Hallowed by thy Name,
Thy kingdom come,
Thy will be done,
On earth as it is in heaven.
Give us this day our daily bread.
And forgive us our trespasses,
As we forgive those
Who trespass against us.
And lead us not into temptation,
But deliver us from evil.
For thine is the kingdom,
And the power, and the glory,
For ever and ever.
Amen

Lord, teach me all that I should know;
In grace and wisdom I may grow;
The more I learn to do Thy will;
The better may I love Thee still.
Amen

Isaac Watts
England 1674–1748

Father, may I so live the life of love this day,
That all those with whom I have anything to do
May be as sure of love in the world
As they are of the sunlight.

Unknown

Ye are the light of the world. A city that is set on a hill cannot be hid.
Neither do men light a candle, and put it under a bushel,
But on a candlestick; and it giveth light unto all that are in the house.
Let your light so shine before men, that they may see your good works,
And glorify your Father which is in heaven.

Matthew 5: 14–16

O thou great Chief,
Light a candle within my heart
That I may see what is therein
And sweep the rubbish from
Thy dwelling place.

An African Girl

Bless, O Lord Jesus, my parents,
And all who love me and take care of me.
Make me loving to them:
Polite and obedient, helpful and kind. Amen

Unknown

13

Lord of all eagerness, Lord of all faith,
Whose strong hands were skilled at the plane and the lathe,
Be there at our labors, and give us, we pray,
Your strength in our hearts, Lord, at the noon of the day.

Jan Struther
1933

Bless This Food
The Noon of the Day

To God who gives our daily bread,
A thankful song we raise;
And Pray that He who sends us food,
May fill our hearts with praise.

Thomas Tallis
England 1505–1585

Some hae meat and canna eat,
And some wad eat that want it.
But we hae meat and we can eat,
And sae the Lord be thankit.

Robert Burns
Scotland 1759–1796

Back of the loaf is the snowy flour,
And back of the flour, the mill;
And back of the mill is the wheat and the shower,
And the sun and the Father's will.

M. D. Babcock
England 1858–1901

The House Upon a Rock

Jesus had only a very short time to teach his apostles and those around them all that he wanted them to know and understand. When he finished teaching one day, to make sure they understood how important the lesson was, He said to them:

> Whoever hears these teachings of mine, and does them, I would liken him to a wise man, who built his house upon a rock *(I think Jesus meant a firm footing, perhaps many rocks held together with mortar or a large slab of bedrock; something very firm and immoveable.)*

> And the rain came down and the floods came and the wind blew and beat upon that house: and it did not fall down, for it was built upon rock.

> And everyone who hears my teachings, and does not obey them is like a foolish man who built his house upon the sand. And the rain came down, and the floods came and the winds blew and beat upon that house: and it fell, and it was a great fall.

> When Jesus had finished the story, the people were amazed at his teaching, for He taught them as one having great authority.

I think Jesus means for us to build our lives like the house of the wise man: on the solid teachings of Jesus, doing things the way He teaches us and treating each other with love and forgiveness, as we would like to be treated. That way the storms of life will not cause us to fall.

We thank you Lord for happy hearts,
For rain and sunny weather;
We thank you Lord for this our food,
And that we are together.

Traditional

Earth who gives to us our food,
Sun who makes it ripe and good,
Dearest earth and dearest sun,
Joy and love for all you have done.

Traditional

Come, Lord Jesus, be our guest;
And let these gifts to us be blessed.
By Thy hand we all are fed;
Thank you, Lord, for daily bread.

Traditional

Feeding the Five Thousand

Jesus had sent his apostles into the towns to preach the gospel and heal the sick. The apostles, when they returned, told Jesus what they had done; He took them to a desert place near Bethsaida. When the people in the area learned where they had gone, they followed Him and Jesus taught and healed them. It was getting late in the day and the twelve apostles asked Jesus to send the crowd away so they could disperse to the town and find places to eat and sleep. I imagine it had been a long, dusty day and they were tired.

> Jesus told the apostles to give the people something to eat, to which the apostles replied, "we have only five loaves and two fishes; we shall have to go buy meat for all these people"—for there were about five thousand. Jesus replied "Have them all sit down in groups of 50." When they had done so, Jesus took the five loaves and two fishes and looking up to heaven, blessed them, broke them and gave them to the disciples to set out for the crowd. And they ate and were filled and the leftovers that were gathered up filled twelve baskets.

I think we learn from this that we are to offer all we have and all we are to God, and when we pray and trust God, even things that seem impossible can happen.

Bless this food to our use, O Lord
And give us thankful hearts,
In Jesus' Name
Amen

Traditional

For food, and all Thy gifts of love,
We give Thee thanks and praise.
Look down, O Father, from above
And bless us all our days.

Traditional

God is great, and God is good
And we thank Him for this food.
By His hand we all are fed;
Thank you Lord for daily bread.

Traditional

We are thankful for this food;
For health and home and all things good;
For the wind and the rain and the sun above;
But most of all, for those we love.

Traditional

I Jesu namn
Till bords vi gå
Välsigna Gud den
Mat vi få. Gud till
Ära, oss till gagn
Så få vi mat
I Jesu namn.

In Jesus' name
To the table we go
God bless the food
We receive. To God
The honor, Us the gain,
So we have food
In Jesus' name.

Swedish Blessing

23

I will lift up mine eyes unto the hills;
From whence cometh my help.
My help cometh from the Lord,
Which made heaven and earth.
He will not suffer thy foot to be moved:
He that keepeth thee will not slumber.
Behold, he that keepeth Israel
Shall neither slumber nor sleep.
The Lord is thy keeper:
The Lord is thy shade upon thy right hand.
The sun shall not smite thee by day,
Nor the moon by night.
The Lord shall preserve thee from all evil:
He shall preserve thy soul.
The Lord shall preserve thy going out, and thy coming in,
From this time forth, and even for evermore.

Psalm 121

Bless O Lord, this fruitful land;
Bless the hands that till the soil;
Bless those who labor to reap the harvest;
Bless the work and creativity of those who prepare our meals.
Let us go out into the world,
Strengthened by the work of all these hands
And filled with the joy of your love,
To do the work you have for us to do
With joy and love and faithfulness.
Amen

Anne Sandall

Make a joyful noise unto the Lord, all the earth:
make a loud noise, and rejoice, and sing praise.
Sing unto the Lord with the harp; with the harp, and the voice of a psalm.
With trumpets and sound of cornet make a
joyful noise before the Lord, the King.
Let the sea roar, and the fullness thereof:
the world, and they that dwell therein.
Let the floods clap their hands:
Let the hills be joyful together
Before the Lord;
For he cometh to judge the earth: with righteousness shall he judge the
world, and the people with equity.

Psalm 98: 4–9

Thou that hast given so much to me,
Give one thing more—a grateful heart:
Not thankful when it pleaseth me,
As if Thy blessings had spare days,
But such a heart
Whose Pulse may be
Thy Praise.

George Herbert
England 1593–1633

Lord of all kindliness, Lord of all grace,
Your hands swift to welcome, your arms to embrace
Be there at our homing and give us, we pray,
Your love in our hearts, Lord, at the eve of the day.

Jan Struther
1933

Bless Our Sleep
The Eve of the Day

I saw a stranger yestreen*,
I put food in the eating place,
Drink in the drinking place,
Music in the listening place,
And in the sacred name of the triune,
He blessed myself and my house,
My cattle and my dear ones,
And the lark said in her song
Often, often, often
Goes the Christ in the stranger's guise.

Iona Community
Scotland

*yestereen In Scotland, yesterday evening

God bless all those that I love;
God bless all those that love me;
God bless all those that love those that I love;
And all those that love those that love me.

From an old New England sampler

I am your lamb, hold me close; guide my feet; lead me home.
In your arms, find repose.
I am your child, still my fears; help my lips sing your praise.
Let your love dry my tears.
You are my Savior; you hear when I pray.
Let my ears hear your call.
Help my will to obey.

Anne Sandall

31

Jesus, grant thy children calm and sweet repose;
With thy tenderest blessings, may our eyelids close.
When the morning wakens, then may we arise,
Pure and fresh and sinless in Thy holy eyes.

In my little bed I lie,
God, my Father, hear my cry;
Please protect me through the night,
Keep me safe till morning light.

Upon the pillow of thy love
My weary head I lay,
Assured that watchers from above
Will round about me stay.

Gentle Jesus,
Open the gates of Heaven for (*name*)
And welcome *him/her*.
I will miss *him/her* but I know You love *him/her*.
I am happy that *he/she* is now with You.
Let that knowledge bring peace and joy
To all who love *him/her*.
Amen

Anne Sandall

Matthew, Mark, Luke, and John
Bless the bed that I lie on.
There are four corners to my bed;
There are four angels at my head;
One to watch and one to pray
And two to bear my soul away.

Traditional

Lord keep us safe this night,
Secure from all our fears;
May angels guard us while we sleep,
Till morning light appears.

The Lord is my shepherd; I shall not want.
He maketh me to lie down in green pastures:
he leadeth me beside the still waters.
He restoreth my soul:
He leadeth me in the paths of righteousness for his name's sake.
Yea, though I walk through the valley of the shadow of death,
I will fear no evil:
For thou art with me; thy rod and thy staff they comfort me.
Thou preparest a table before me in the presence of mine enemies:
Thou anointest my head with oil; my cup runneth over.
Surely goodness and mercy shall follow me all the days of my life:
And I will dwell in the house of the Lord for ever.

Psalm 23

Jesus, tender Shepherd, hear me;
Bless thy little lamb tonight:
Through the darkness be thou near me,
Keep me safe till morning light.
All this day thy hand has led me,
And I thank thee for thy care;
Thou hast warmed me, clothed, and fed me;
Listen to my evening prayer.
Let my sins be all forgiven;
Bless the friends I love so well;
Take us all at last to heaven,
Happy there with Thee to dwell.
Amen

Mary Duncan
1839

Oh Lord Jesus, whose earthly father was a carpenter,
Whose disciples were fishermen and tax collectors,
You have taught us that all work is acceptable if
It is intended for Your honor.
Help us in all our endeavors,
To do everything for your honor and glory,
To do it all to the best of our ability,
To harm no person by what we do,
To do no harm to this beautiful world
You have created for our earthly home.
Help us to do nothing which will cause someone to sin,
But in all things, follow that which makes for peace,
And serves to lift us all closer to you.
In Jesus' Name
Amen

Anne Sandall

O Lord, support us all the day long, until
The shadows lengthen, and the evening comes,
And the busy world is hushed, and the fever
Of life is over, and our work is done.
Then, in Thy mercy, grant us a safe lodging,
And a holy rest, and peace at the last.
Amen

Book of Common Prayer
1979

These things, good Lord, that we pray for,
Give us Thy grace to labour for.

Sir Thomas More
England 1478–1535

O God, from whom all holy desires, all good counsels,
And all just works do proceed;
Give unto thy servants that peace which the world cannot give;
That our hearts may be set to obey thy commandments,
And also that by thee, we, being defended from the fear of our enemies,
May pass our time in rest and quietness;
Through the merits of Jesus Christ our Savior.
Amen

Book of Common Prayer
1928

Lighten our darkness, we beseech thee, O Lord;
And by thy great mercy defend us from all perils and dangers of this night;
For the love of thy only son, our Savior, Jesus Christ.
Amen

Book of Common Prayer
1928

Lord, make us instruments of your peace.
Where there is hatred, let us sow love;
Where there is injury, pardon;
Where there is discord, union;
Where there is darkness, light;
Where there is sadness, joy.
Grant that we may not so much seek to be consoled
As to console;
To be understood as to understand;
To be loved as to love.
For it is in giving that we receive;
It is in pardoning that
We are pardoned;
And it is in dying that we are born to eternal life.
Amen

Book of Common Prayer
1979

Lord of all gentleness, Lord of all calm,
Whose voice is contentment, whose presence is balm,
Be there at our sleeping, and give us, we pray,
Your peace in our hearts, Lord, at the end of the day.

Jan Struther
1933

For All Our Blessings
The End of the Day

Acknowledgments

Every effort has been made to assign proper credits for selections; if any have been omitted where due, we will happily include them in subsequent editions. We thank the following publishers, individuals, and organizations for their kind permission to reprint these prayers:

Prayers, Praises, and Thanksgivings; comp. by Sandol Stoddard; page 27, "Thou that hast given so much to me..."; page 13, "O Thou great chief..."; page 3, "This morning, God..."; page 30, "I saw a stranger..."; Published by Dial Books, Copyright 1992.

The Book of Common Prayer (1979) of the Episcopal Church, USA; page v, "O Lord, in your Holy Spirit" adaptation; page 41, "Lord, make us instruments of your Peace..."; page 39, "O Lord, support us..."; Published by the Church Hymnal Corporation, New York; certified September 1979.

The Book of Common Prayer (1928) of the Episcopal Church, USA; page 40, "Lighten our darkness..."; page 40, "O God from whom all holy desires..."; page 10, "Our Father, who art in heaven..."; The Seabury Press, Greenwich, Connecticut.

The Hymnal 1940; New York pages 1, 15, 29, 43, "Lord of all Hopefulness..."; Text: Jan Struther (Joyce Placzek, nee Torrens), 1901-1953, Oxford University Press; page 37, "Jesus, Tender Shepherd Hear me..."; Mary Duncan 1839; Published by the Church Hymnal Corporation, New York, Copyright 1940.

Hymns and Tunes for Public and Private Worship; page 5, "My God was with me all the night ..."; page 35, "Lord, keep us safe this night... "; page 32, "Jesus, grant thy children..."; page 33, "Upon the pillow of thy love..."; Published by Mennonite Publishing Company Elkhart, Indiana 1890.

Children's Prayers from Other Lands; comp. by Dorothy G. Spicer; page 33, "In my little bed..." ; Association Press, Copyright 1955.

Wild Goose Publications, Iona Community, Glasgow, Scotland, page 3, "This morning God..." was first heard during a visit to the Abbey on the Isle of Iona; though no written version has been found. We are indebted to Sandol Stoddard for making it available and Wild Goose Publications for their help in trying to locate the origin. Also from the Iona Community via Prayers, Praises and Thanksgivings, page 30, "I saw a stranger..." It is the Celtic rune of hospitality and is sometimes used in the Welcome service at the Iona Abbey. The Iona Abbey Worship Book, 2001; Wild Goose Publications, Glasgow G2 3DH; Scotland www.ionabooks.com.

Armenian Apostolic Church, Lebanon; page 5, "O God creator of light..."

Forward Movement Publications "I believe in God above..." quoted by Dr. Manderbach in the Foreword.

Be Thou Faithful! Words of Advice, Comfort and Cheer to the Confirmed; L. A. Johnston, D.D.; page 2, "With humble heart and tongue..."; Lutheran Augustana Book Concern, Rock Island, Illinois; Given to Irene Carlson Sandall by Pastor Loudin on the occasion of her confirmation, May 28, 1916.

The Holy Bible; Authorized (King James) Version; page 12, Matthew 5: 14-16; page 24, Psalm 121; page 26, Psalm 98: 4-9; page 36, Psalm 23.

Index Of First Lines

My Special Thanksgivings

My Special Intentions

Other Favorite Prayers

How Your Book Was Created

The typeface used in the text is Carmina. It was designed by Gudrun Zapf von Hesse sometime after 1954 for Bitstream Inc. In 1991 Ms. Von Hesse was awarded the Frederic W. Goudy Award, the distinguished award in the field of book and type design in the United States.

The typeface used on the cover and for the chapter titles was first seen in *A Treasury of Authentic Art Nouveau Alphabets*, *Decorative Initials*, *Monograms*, *Frames and Ornaments*, plate 7, Alphabet Von Georges Lemmen. The book was edited by Ludwig Petzendorfer and published by Dover Publications. The font was purchased under the name Bucephalus. David Nalle, founder and lead designer of original fonts and adapter of historical source material for *The Scriptorium*, may have used the Dover publication when creating the font.

My thanks to McClain's Printmaking Supply of Portland, OR for their wonderful supplies and friendly advice.

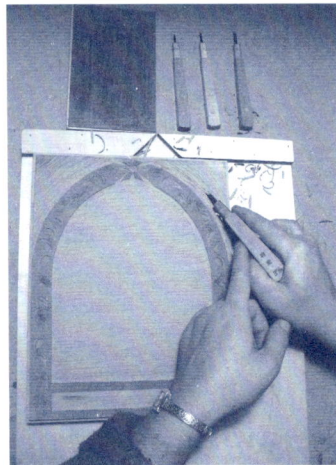

Carving the block.

Ready to print.

Examining the prints.